FOOTBALL

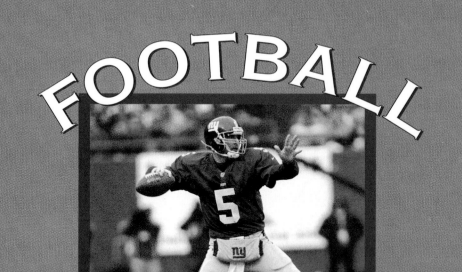

A TRUE BOOK®

by

Mike Kennedy

Children's Press®
A Division of Scholastic Inc.

New York Toronto London Auckland Sydney
Mexico City New Delhi Hong Kong
Danbury, Connecticut

A referee measuring for a first down during a youth football league game

Reading Consultant
Nanci R. Vargus, *Ed.D.*
Teacher in Residence
University of Indianapolis
Indianapolis, Indiana

Library of Congress Cataloging-in-Publication Data

Kennedy, Mike (Mike William), 1965-
    Football / Mike Kennedy.
        p. cm. — (True books)
    Includes bibliographical references (p.) and index.
    ISBN 0-516-22336-4 (lib bdg.)   0-516-29373-7 (pbk.)
Football—Juvenile literature. [I. Football.] I. Title. II. True book.

GV950.7 .K46 2002
796.332—dc21

                                              2001017183

Contents

A ball carrier bursts into the clear.

How Football Began

Would it surprise you to learn that football was not "born" in the United States? It actually was based on the English sport of rugby—known long ago as the "carrying game."

Rugby, like football, is a game played by two teams on a large field. The team with the

American football grew out of the sport of rugby (above).

ball tries to advance into its opponent's territory. The other team tires to defend its "turf" by stopping its opponent or taking away the ball. There are a variety of ways to score, both by running the ball and kicking it.

Rugby made its way to the United States in the 1800s and quickly became popular with college students. Over the years, the rules gradually changed until the sport looked more and more like the game we know as football.

In 1880, a Yale University student named Walter Camp suggested using a "line of scrimmage"—an imaginary **barrier** that separates the offense and defense. This was

Players taking their positions on either side of the line of scrimmage in a 1902 football game

very different from rugby, which allowed players from both teams to crowd around the ball without any strict **boundaries**.

Football faced a big crisis in 1904. Games were very rough. Players wore no helmets and

little padding. President
Theodore Roosevelt threatened
to **ban** the sport if colleges did
not make it safer. Two years
later, the forward pass was made
part of the game. Now a player
could throw the ball down the

By the early 1900s, some players had begun
to wear helmets. It would be years, however,
before teams mastered the forward pass.

field to a teammate. The forward pass "opened up" the field and cut down on the mass tackling that had caused so many injuries.

During this time, some players began competing as professionals. It was not until 1920, however, that the first true "league" started. This organization is still with us: the National Football League (NFL). To attract new fans during the Great Depression,

Exciting NFL action from 1948

the NFL adopted new rules to increase scoring. One called for a smaller ball, which has been in use ever since.

First and Ten

In football, the team that scores more points is the winner. On each play, eleven players from each team line up against one another on a rectangular field with goal posts at each end.

In the NFL, college, and high school, the playing field

measures 100 yards (91 meters) long and 160 feet (49 m) wide. There are also two 10-yard (9-m) "end zones" at each end. The line that separates each end

An overhead view of an NFL stadium

zone from the playing field is the "goal line." The line that runs the length of each side of the playing field is the side-line. The "50-yard line" splits the field in two equal halves.

Every game starts with a kickoff, in which one team

14

Every football game begins with a kickoff.

boots the ball to the other. The team that receives the ball goes on offense first. In the NFL and college, players normally are asked to play either offense or defense. At some levels, however, players go "both ways."

A quarterback
stretches for
extra yardage as
the defense
brings him down.

On offense, a team gets four chances, or "downs," to move the ball at least 10 yards. Every time it does so, it gets four new downs. If the team on offense fails to move the ball 10 yards in four downs, the other team gets the ball. Now that team will try to move the ball—in the

On fourth down, the team on offense normally punts the ball down the field.

opposite direction. That's why teams usually kick, or "punt," the ball down the field to their opponent on fourth down. This forces the other team backwards before it starts on offense.

To advance the ball, the offense can either run with it or pass it. To run the ball, players

An offensive lineman blocks a defender to clear a path for his running back.

on offense must block defenders to create openings for a teammate who has the ball. That ball carrier then tries to race downfield before being tackled or pushed across the sideline and out of bounds. When either one

A quarterback releases a pass before being tackled (left) and a receiver reaches high to catch a pass (right).

happens, the action ends. On a pass play, the passer must stay behind the line of scrimmage and then throw the ball down the field to a teammate. If the pass is caught, the receiver becomes just like a ball carrier on a running play.

If a player loses the ball, it is considered a "fumble," which anyone can **recover**. When the defense pounces on it, a "turnover" results. Now that team goes on offense. The same thing happens when a defender **intercepts** a pass. If either an offensive or defensive player drops a pass before having control of the ball, however, it is ruled "incomplete." This means play stops immediately.

A defender knocking the ball loose from a receiver (top), a defender recovering a fumble (middle), and a defender intercepting a pass (bottom)

A touchdown is worth six points (above). A field goal is worth three points (right).

The offense tries to score touchdowns (six points) by carrying the ball across its opponent's goal line and into the end zone. It also can score a field goal (three points) by kicking the ball through the goal posts. After a touchdown, the offense either kicks an extra point or tries the riskier two-point conversion. "Going for two" means you get one play from the 3-yard line to get into the end zone.

The defense tries to stop the offense with its own schemes.

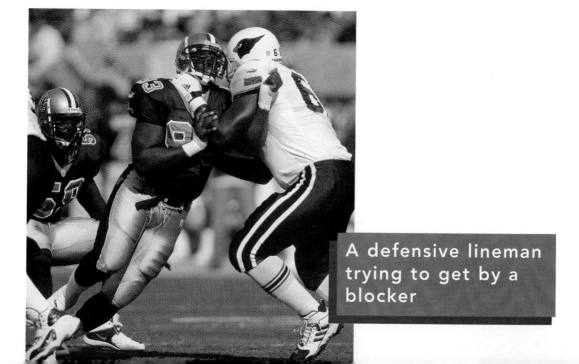

A defensive lineman trying to get by a blocker

Defenders either cover specific areas or "zones" of the field, or guard opponents one-on-one. The defense also can score two points by tackling a ball carrier in his own end zone for a "safety."

Several referees wearing black-and-white striped shirts enforce the rules. When an official spots an **infraction**, the guilty team is **penalized**. Examples of penalties include offensive holding (grabbing a

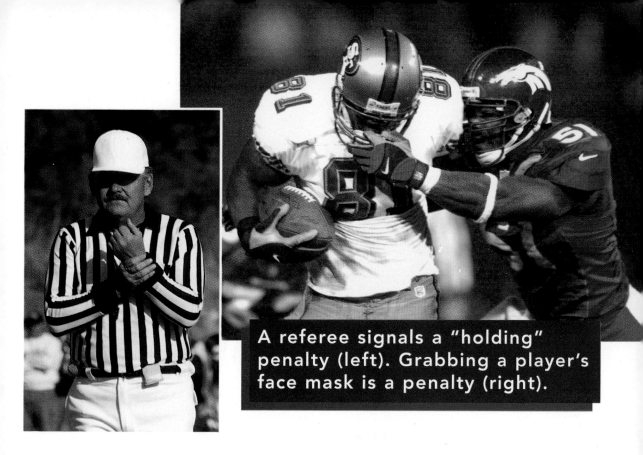

A referee signals a "holding" penalty (left). Grabbing a player's face mask is a penalty (right).

defender during a block), defensive pass interference (making contact with a receiver while a pass is in the air), and face masking (grabbing a player's face mask).

Huddle Up

Before every down, the players on offense and defense huddle to plan **strategy**. Do you know the positions on each side of the ball?

The quarterback directs the offense. It takes a sharp mind and an **accurate** arm to play this position. Quarterbacks handle the ball on just about every

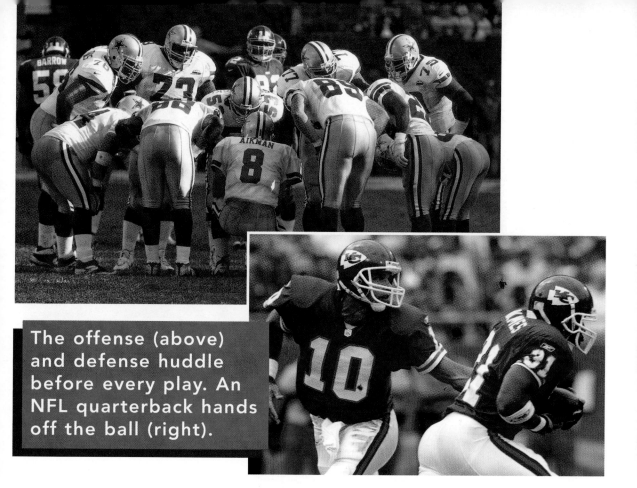

The offense (above) and defense huddle before every play. An NFL quarterback hands off the ball (right).

play. They hand off the ball on running plays and throw nearly every pass. Good quarterbacks can "read" what the defense is going to do, and take advantage of weaknesses they see.

The best running backs are quick, nimble, and fearless.

Running backs line up behind the quarterback, and usually get the ball on running plays. The best running backs are strong, fast, and difficult to tackle. On passing plays, they either block for the quarter-back or run to an open spot and hope the ball is thrown to them.

On most passes, the quarter-back's main targets are the tight end, split end, and flanker. Above all, these receivers need sure hands. Speed and being able to change direction quickly also help. Tight ends usually line up next to

A receiver leaving his feet to make a great catch

the linemen, so they have to be good blockers, too.

The linemen—two tackles, two guards, and the center—are the offense's unsung heroes. They never get to touch the ball, except for the center. He starts every play by "snapping" the ball between his legs to the quarterback. Offensive linemen protect the players who carry the ball, so they must be powerful, quick, and smart.

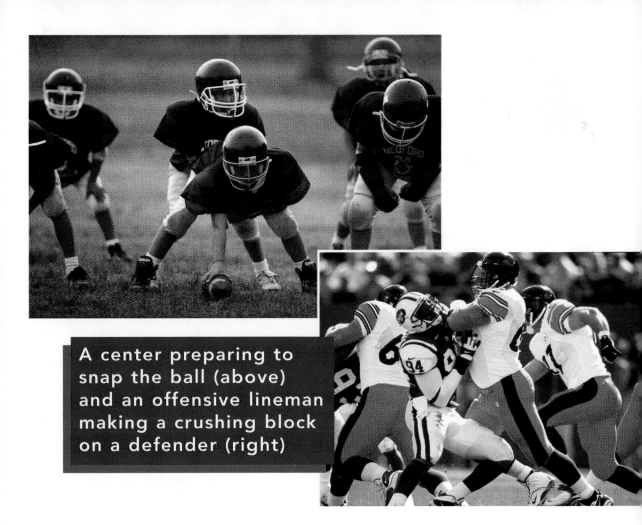

A center preparing to snap the ball (above) and an offensive lineman making a crushing block on a defender (right)

Defensive tackles and ends make up the defensive line. Their job is to overpower the offensive line, and make it hard to run or pass.

A linebacker tackling a ball carrier (above) and a cornerback (in yellow helmet) breaking up a pass attempt (right)

Linebackers are the next tier of defenders. Good ones have a "nose" for the football. They can figure out what play the offense is running, and then stop the ball carrier with a sure tackle.

The "secondary" is the last line of defense. Cornerbacks often cover the flanker and split end one-on-one. Safeties usually are allowed to roam freely. All four members of the secondary may join the attack, as long as no receivers are open down field.

The punter and place-kicker are "specialists" whose best weapons are their legs and feet. They take the field only when their skills are needed.

Head Honcho

George Halas, longtime head coach of the Chicago Bears

Who sets the game plan for a football team? The head coach, of course. Some coaches, in fact, are more famous than their players. Here are four of the greatest coaches ever: George Halas, Knute Rockne, Vince Lombardi, and Joe Paterno.

Green Bay Packers head coach Vince Lombardi celebrating a championship win

Notre Dame coach Knute Rockne (center) surrounded by his team in 1930

Penn State coach Joe Paterno pacing the sidelines during a game

Suiting Up

Football is a game of collisions. Players at all levels must wear proper protective gear.

The helmet is the most important piece of equipment. It has a hard shell and thick padding that protects your head. A face mask is attached to the front of the helmet. It safeguards your eyes, nose, cheeks, and chin.

A football player should always wear a protective helmet (left) and shoulder pads (right).

Plastic mouth guards are required in most leagues, as well. Shoulder pads are necessary, too. They rest on top of your shoulders and have padding that runs down the upper part of your chest and back. There are also special pads that cushion the blow on your ribs, hips, thighs, and knees.

You wear all of this equipment—except your helmet—under your uniform pants and jersey. Putting on your jersey can be difficult. It has to stretch over your shoulder pads. And remember to take off your helmet first!

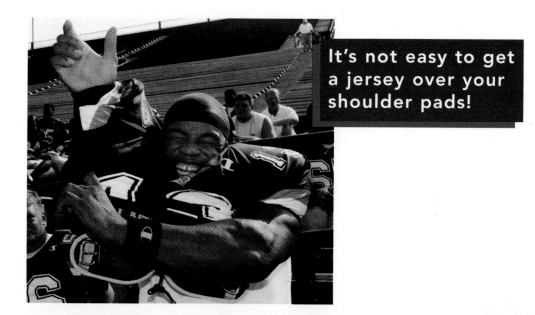

It's not easy to get a jersey over your shoulder pads!

Touchdown!

Life in the National Football League is not easy. The NFL has only 32 teams. To grab a roster spot, you must train year-round, memorize playbooks the size of phone books, and perform in front of thousands of screaming fans.

From junior football to the NFL, there is no better feeling than scoring a touchdown.

Most NFL players learned the game as children. At age five, kids become **eligible** for "junior" football leagues such

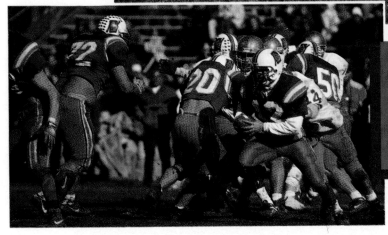

A "junior" league football game (above) and a high-school football game (left)

as Pop Warner. For many players, this is their first taste of organized football with tackling.

By the time kids become teenagers, many already have

begun to play high-school football. Freshmen usually have their own team. Sophomores, juniors, and seniors compete for playing time on the varsity.

Some players continue their careers in college. The very best receive **scholarships**. The top college players are selected in the NFL draft. Those who do not make a team often join other professional leagues. They have to work even harder if they want another chance to play in the NFL.

Gridiron Greats

Here are ten players who changed football:

Pudge Heffelfinger, lineman, pro: 1892-97
Teams did not pay their players until Pudge came along with his daring style of play.

Pudge Heffelfinger

Jim Thorpe, running back, defensive back, & kicker, pro: 1915-28

Thorpe was an American Indian and the most amazing athlete football has ever seen.

Jim Thorpe

Red Grange, running back, pro: 1925-34

The game's greatest open-field runner, the "Galloping Ghost" gave pro football a huge boost by signing with the Chicago Bears.

Red Grange

Don Hutson, wide receiver & defensive back, pro: 1935-45

Blessed with soft hands and great moves, he "invented" the position of wide receiver.

Don Hutson

Sammy Baugh, quarterback, defensive back, & punter, pro: 1937-52

Slingin' Sammy was the NFL's first superstar signal-caller, and probably the best punter ever.

Sammy Baugh

Johnny Unitas

Johnny Unitas, quarterback, pro: 1956-73

"Johnny U" was tough and talented—and always at his best when his team needed him the most.

Jim Brown, running back, pro: 1957-65

He combined the size of a linebacker with the speed of a wideout to become the most devastating runner in football history.

Jim Brown

Deacon Jones, defensive lineman, pro: 1961-74

The leader of the "Fearsome Foursome," he introduced fans—and opposing passers—to the quarterback sack.

Deacon Jones

Joe Montana, quarterback, pro: 1979-94

No ordinary Joe, he took the modern passing game to a new level.

Joe Montana

Lawrence Taylor, linebacker, pro: 1981-93

An offense's worst nightmare, LT made linebacker the most glamorous position on defense.

Lawrence Taylor

To Find Out More

Here are some additional resources to help you learn more about football:

Books

Barber, Phil. **Superstars of the NFL.** Andrews McMeel Publishing, 1998.

Neft, David; Cohen, Richard and Korch, Rick. **The Sports Encyclopedia Pro Football.** St. Martin's Griffin, Annual.

Stewart, Mark. **Football: A History of the Gridiron Game.** Franklin Watts, 1998.

Sullivan, George. **All About Football.** G.P. Putnam's Sons, 1987.

Organizations and Online Sites

College Football Hall of Fame

http:www. collegefootball.org

Provides information on the legends of the college game as well as current players on track to join them.

Dick Butkus Football Network

http://www.dickbutkus.com

Includes extensive information about Pop Warner football.

National Football League

http://www.nfl.com

Offers the latest scores, standings, and news on every player in the NFL. Also includes a special section for kids.

Pro Football Hall of Fame

http://www. profootballhof.com

Find out about the greatest players in NFL history and learn about the history of the professional game.

Important Words

accurate precise

ban to stop something from happening

barrier something that blocks the way or keeps things apart

boundaries places that mark a limit; dividing lines

eligible qualified to be chosen

infraction in football, when a player does something that is not allowed

intercepts in football, when a defensive player catches a pass

penalized punished for breaking a rule

recover in football, to get control the ball after a fumble

scholarship money given to a student to pay for his or her education

strategy well-thought-out plan to achieve a goal

Index

Meet the Author

Mike Kennedy is a freelance sportswriter whose work has ranged from Super Bowl coverage to historical research and analysis. He has profiled athletes in virtually every sport, including Peyton Manning, Bernie Williams, and Allen Iverson. He is a graduate of Franklin & Marshall College in Lancaster, Pennsylvania.

Mike has contributed his expertise to other books by Scholastic, including *Auto Racing: A History of Fast Cars and Fearless Drivers*. He has authored four other sports True Books, including *Basketball* and *Baseball*.